KUMITE 2

BEST KARATE 4

Kumite 2

M. Nakayama

KODANSHA INTERNATIONAL LTD.

Tokyo, New York & San Francisco

Front cover photo by Keizō Kaneko; demonstration photos by Yoshinao Murai.

Distributed in the United States by Kodansha International/USA Ltd. through Harper & Row, Publishers, Inc., 10 East 53rd Street, New York, New York 10022.

Published by Kodansha International Ltd., 12-21, Otowa 2-chome, Bunkyo-ku, Tokyo 112 and Kodansha International/USA Ltd., 10 East 53rd Street, New York, New York 10022 and 44 Montgomery Street, San Francisco, California 94104. Copyright © 1979 by Kodansha International Ltd. All rights reserved. Printed in Japan.

LCC 77–74829
ISBN 0–87011–359–3
ISBN 4–7700–0686–1 (in Japan)

First edition, 1979
Third printing, 1983

CONTENTS

Dedicated
to my teacher
GICHIN FUNAKOSHI
and to
MINORU MIYATA

INTRODUCTION

The past decade has seen a great increase in the popularity of karate-dō throughout the world. Among those who have been attracted to it are college students and teachers, artists, businessmen and civil servants. It has come to be practiced by policemen and members of Japan's Self-defense Forces. In a number of universities, it has become a compulsory subject, and that number is increasing yearly.

Along with the increase in popularity, there have been certain unfortunate and regrettable interpretations and performances. For one thing, karate has been confused with the so-called Chinese-style boxing, and its relationship with the original Okinawan *Te* has not been sufficiently understood. There are also people who have regarded it as a mere show, in which two men attack each other savagely, or the contestants battle each other as though it were a form of boxing in which the feet are used, or a man shows off by breaking bricks or other hard objects with his head, hand or foot.

If karate is practiced solely as a fighting technique, this is cause for regret. The fundamental techniques have been developed and perfected through long years of study and practice, but to make any effective use of these techniques, the spiritual aspect of this art of self-defense must be recognized and must play the predominant role. It is gratifying to me to see that there are those who understand this, who know that karate-dō is a purely Oriental martial art, and who train with the proper attitude.

To be capable of inflicting devastating damage on an opponent with one blow of the fist or a single kick has indeed been the objective of this ancient Okinawan martial art. But even the practitioners of old placed stronger emphasis on the spiritual side of the art than on the techniques. Training means training of body and spirit, and, above all else, one should treat his opponent courteously and with the proper etiquette. It is not enough to fight with all one's power; the real objective in karate-dō is to do so for the sake of justice.

Gichin Funakoshi, a great master of karate-dō, pointed out repeatedly that the first purpose in pursuing this art is the nurturing of a sublime spirit, a spirit of humility. Simultaneously, power sufficient to destroy a ferocious wild animal with a single blow should be developed. Becoming a true follower of karate-dō is possible only when one attains perfection in these two aspects, the one spiritual, the other physical.

Karate as an art of self-defense and karate as a means of improving and maintaining health has long existed. During the past twenty years, a new activity has been explored and is coming to the fore. This is *sports karate.*

In sports karate, contests are held for the purpose of determining the ability of the participants. This needs emphasizing, for here again there is cause for regret. There is a tendency to place too much emphasis on winning contests, and those who do so neglect the practice of fundamental techniques, opting instead to attempt jiyū kumite at the earliest opportunity.

Emphasis on winning contests cannot help but alter the fundamental techniques a person uses and the practice he engages in. Not only that, it will result in a person's being incapable of executing a strong and effective technique, which, after all, is the unique characteristic of karate-dō. The man who begins jiyū kumite prematurely—without having practiced fundamentals sufficiently—will soon be overtaken by the man who has trained in the basic techniques long and diligently. It is, quite simply, a matter of haste makes waste. There is no alternative to learning and practicing basic techniques and movements step by step, stage by stage.

If karate competitions are to be held, they must be conducted under suitable conditions and in the proper spirit. The desire to win a contest is counterproductive, since it leads to a lack of seriousness in learning the fundamentals. Moreover, aiming for a savage display of strength and power in a contest is totally undesirable. When this happens, courtesy toward the opponent is forgotten, and this is of prime importance in any expression of karate. I believe this matter deserves a great deal of reflection and self-examination by both instructors and students.

To explain the many and complex movements of the body, it has been my desire to present a fully illustrated book with an up-to-date text, based on the experience in this art that I have acquired over a period of forty-six years. This hope is being realized by the publication of the *Best Karate* series, in which earlier writings of mine have been totally revised with the help and encouragement of my readers. This new series explains in detail what karate-dō is in language made as simple as possible, and I sincerely hope that it will be of help to followers of karate-dō. I hope also that karateka in many countries will be able to understand each other better through this series of books.

Deciding who is the winner and who is the loser is not the ultimate objective. Karate-dō is a martial art for the development of character through training, so that the karateka can surmount any obstacle, tangible or intangible.

Karate-dō is an empty-handed art of self-defense in which the arms and legs are systematically trained and an enemy attacking by surprise can be controlled by a demonstration of strength like that of using actual weapons.

Karate-dō is exercise through which the karateka masters all body movements, such as bending, jumping and balancing, by learning to move limbs and body backward and forward, left and right, up and down, freely and uniformly.

The techniques of karate-dō are well controlled according to the karateka's will power and are directed at the target accurately and spontaneously.

The essence of karate techniques is *kime*. The meaning of *kime* is an explosive attack to the target using the appropriate technique and maximum power in the shortest time possible. (Long ago, there was the expression *ikken hissatsu*, meaning "to kill with one blow," but to assume from this that killing is the objective is dangerous and incorrect. It should be remembered that the karateka of old were able to practice *kime* daily and in dead seriousness by using the makiwara.)

Kime may be accomplished by striking, punching or kicking, but also by blocking. A technique lacking *kime* can never be regarded as true karate, no matter how great the resemblance to karate. A contest is no exception; however, it is against the rules to make contact because of the danger involved.

Sun-dome means to arrest a technique just before contact with the target (one *sun*, about three centimeters). But not carrying a technique through to *kime* is not true karate, so the question is how to reconcile the contradiction between *kime* and *sun-dome*. The answer is this: establish the target slightly in front of the opponent's vital point. It can then be hit in a controlled way with maximum power, without making contact.

Training transforms various parts of the body into weapons to be used freely and effectively. The quality necessary to accomplish this is self-control. To become a victor, one must first overcome his own self.

Organization of volumes 3 and 4

Volumes 3 and 4 of the Best Karate series give a selection of techniques, tactics and strategy applicable in kumite training. These are organized, chapter by chapter, so as to give guidance to the beginner for improvement. I have used a large number of photographs but rather few words. I hope you will study both with care and train with diligence.

Techniques used in kumite are demonstrated by instructors of the Japan Karate Association as follows:

Volume 3:

Sen no Sen	Takeshi Ōishi, Shunsuke Takahashi
Go no Sen	Norihiko Iida, Yoshiharu Ōsaka
Types of Kicking	Masaaki Ueki, Mikio Yahara
Striking in Close Combat	Keigo Abe, Mikio Yahara
Kicking in Close Combat	Katsunori Tsuyama, Eishige Matsukura
Rotation, Tai-sabaki, Throwing	Tetsuhiko Asai, Yoshiharu Ōsaka
Two-level Attack	Hirokazu Kanazawa, Yoshiharu Ōsaka

This volume:

Kuzushi, Leg Sweep	Keinosuke Enoeda, Fujikiyo Ōmura
Changing Techniques	Toru Yamaguchi, Yoshiki Satō
Cutting Kick	Masahiko Tanaka, Masao Kawazoe
Response to Punch or Kick	Masao Kawazoe, Yoshiharu Ōsaka
Last-chance Technique	Mikio Yahara, Takashi Naito
Continuous Techniques	Hiroshi Shōji, Toru Yamaguchi
Blocking Kime	Masatoshi Nakayama, Yoshiharu Ōsaka

To help the karateka to understand the spirit and mental attitude of the martial arts, there are selections from:

Heihōka densho by Yagyū Munenori
Gorin no sho by Miyamoto Musashi
Ittōsai sensei kempō sho by Kotōda Yahei

1
KUMITE

MEANING AND TYPES

The Meaning of Kumite

Kumite is a method of training in which the offensive and defensive techniques learned in the kata are given pratical application. The opponents are face to face.

The importance of kata to kumite cannot be overemphasized. If techniques are used unnaturally or in a forced way, posture will break down. And if the kata techniques become confused when applied, no improvement in kumite can be expected. In other words, improvement in kumite depends directly on improvement in kata; the two go together like hand in glove. It is a mistake to emphasize one at the expense of the other. This is a point to be careful about when practicing kumite.

The Types of Kumite

Basic kumite, jiyū ippon kumite and jiyū kumite are the three types of kumite.

Basic kumite

In this most elementary form of kumite, the opponents take a fixed distance from each other and the target area is agreed on beforehand. They then alternately practice attacking and blocking. This may be done as a single attack and block— *ippon kumite*—or a series of five—*gohon kumite* (also three, *sambon kumite*). (See Vol. 1, pp. 112—20.)

Jiyū ippon kumite and jiyū kumite

The late Minoru Miyata was my classmate and a colleague of mine since the founding of the Japan Karate Association. From his long years of experience, he held a clearly defined view of jiyū ippon kumite and jiyū kumite. Since he was a man whose capabilities were highly evaluated by others and one in whom I had very great confidence, I would like to quote him on this subject.

The method of ippon jiyū kumite is this. Both men take a *kamae* freely at an optional distance. [*Kamae*, posture, specifically that of the torso and arms.] Announcing the area he is aiming for, the attacker attacks decisively. Against this the blocker freely uses techniques he has mastered and counterattacks at once. This is a training method; the purpose is to put into actual practice the techniques of offense and defense. This is *jissen* (actual fighting) kumite.

In this way, the attacker, gauging *maai* and *kokyū* (breathing) and making use of feints and so on, takes advantage of any opening and with good timing develops his attacking strength. The blocker, advancing, retreating or executing *tai-sabaki* to left or right, uses his techniques in any direction and counterattacks. Because it involves methods of attack and defense in all directions, *kokyū, maai, tai-sabaki*, shifting the center of gravity, blocking-finishing in one breath, jiyū ippon kumite is an extremely important method for forging techniques.

There is this way of thinking about jiyū ippon kumite. If after attacking, the attacker deceives the blocker and continues to attack, or if he attacks without announcing his intention by turning the blocker's counterattack against him, this training method will become jiyū kumite. This preliminary step to jiyū kumite requires great skill, so it cannot be recommended to beginners, whose techniques will break down and become ineffective. Only for the skilled is this a good method of cultivating true sight, the sixth sense of attack and defense. [See Vol 2, p. 101.]

The tendency recently is to advance to jiyū kumite prematurely, and the result of this—*kime* lacking intense, strong power—is seen far too often, because the participants in contests lack sufficient training in fundamentals and kata. This approach is defective, but I believe it is on the increase. To correct this, instead of taking jiyū ippon kumite as the preliminary step to jiyū kumite, it is of the utmost necessity in the first place to master strong techniques one by one through correct training and, at the same, *maai, kokyū, tai-sabaki*, and so on. Then ippon kumite can be the gateway to jiyū kumite.

Judō has its *randori*, karate-dō its jiyū kumite, to be engaged in without prearrangement. A number of techniques and targets are prohibited. With due regard for this point, it is a free form of *jissen*.

From ancient days when techniques were secret and practiced individually, kata were at the core of training and reached an extremely high level of meaning. Today's karate-dō is also training through kata. As for kumite, basic prearranged kumite was a form of training from a fairly long time ago, but it was only when karate began to thrive in universities and other places in the late 1920s that jiyū kumite was introduced. Training through gohon kumite gained momentum, and this lead to *shizen* (natural) and *jiyū* (free) kumite. Jiyū kumite appeared officially for the first time on a public program in 1936, when a tournament was held commemorating the establishment of the Japan Student Karate-dō Federation. Compared with judō and kendō, this was a late start, and with the inevitable development of sports karate, much deeper research in jiyū kumite must be done.

Essential to training through jiyū kumite are *kamaekata, tachikata, me no tsukekata, maai* and *waza o hodokosu kōki.*

1. *Kamaekata,* posture, specifically of the upper body

Kamaekata must be such as to permit movement in any direction of attack or defense. With the torso in *hanmi,* stand straight but with the feeling that the hips are ever so slightly lowered. Hold your head correctly, inclining neither up nor down, nor to right or left. The forward arm, slightly bent and protecting the side of the body should point between the opponent's nose and upper lip. The back arm should be bent and near the solar plexus. At this time, there should be no unnecessary power in such places as the elbows and the pit of the stomach. This becomes the posture of readiness, with the center of gravity in its natural position.

2. *Tachikata,* stance

Stand lightly, with your feet drawn slightly inward and a little bit closer together than in the front stance or rooted stance. Let the knees bend a little, and let the legs support the body weight equally. Power should be in the soles and toes, but the heels should feel as distant from the floor as the thickness of a sheet of paper. Stand lightly, keeping your composure.

3. *Me no tsukekata,* fixing the eyes

If you fasten your eyes on the opponent's face, you will lose sight of other things. When you are watching for his kick, you will not see his upper body. You must see all, from the top of his head to his toes. To take the measure of the opponent in front of you clearly, let your eyes feel as though they were looking at a distance object.

4. *Maai,* distance

. When face to face with an opponent, the point of greatest importance in fighting strategy is distance. From a practical point of view, *maai* is the distance from which one can advance one step and deliver a decisive punch or kick; reciprocally, it is the distance from which can withdraw one step and protect himself from attack.

Maai differs to a greater or lesser extent according to individual physique and technique, but ideally it means to have the opponent away from you and to be close to him. Distancing has an important meaning in deciding victory or defeat, so it is very important to study and master advantageous *maai.*

5. *Waza o hodokoso kōki,* the psychological moment to execute a technique

Whether attacking by seizing the initiative earlier [*sen*

no sen] or seizing the initiative later (*go no sen*), execution of a technique will have no effect unless advantage is taken of an opening. These are of three kinds: a mental opening, an opening in *kamae* and an opening in movements. The following pertains to the latter.

A. At the start of the opponent's technique. When the opponent, seeing an opening, begins his movement, at the very onset attack directly and instantly. His mind will be on his attack, and his defense insufficient. In that brief time, there can easily be an opening.

B. When the attack comes. When you are attacked, or or when there is a continuous attack that you block, and the opponent's strategic aims are exhausted and his techniques stop, attack.

C. When the mind is motionless. In the martial arts, there are strict warnings about being taken by surprise, being doubtful or vacillating. At the time a kick or punch is imminent, if one is seized by doubt or flinches in the face of the opponent's spirit, he will vacillate about launching his own attack, the body will stiffen, and a mental opening will occur. In this instant, there is a good possibility for a sudden, successful attack.

D. Creating an opening. When there is no opening on either side, a feint may be employed to distract the opponent. For example, a diversionary movement of the foot can draw his attention downward, making an attack to his upper body possible. There are many ways of doing this with the hand or foot, but if it is done clumsily, the opponent can find an opening. In practice, you must have good control of your own power and punch or kick with dead seriousness. One way is to execute continuous techniques that leave the opponent no room for counterattack. Then when his posture crumbles creating an opening, launch an instantaneous and decisive attack.

The above points should be studied carefully while practicing jiyū kumite. Although I repeat myself, I say again that in jiyū kumite, techniques are apt to end up in disarray. Therefore, training must be coordinated with kata, ippon jiyū kumite, etc., and great care must be taken to really learn fundamentals and to master strong techniques before all else.

In kumite training, each person practices each type of kumite according to his own level of progress. It is therefore necessary to fully understand the distinctive features of the various types and to practice with the objectives clearly in mind.

Gohon kumite (or *sambon kumite*)

1. The objective is to become proficient in the use of the formal, fundamental techniques of attack and defense. This means learning and refining accurate punches kicks and blocks and practicing fundamental leg movements (*unsoku*).

2. More advanced students should also master blocking, *tai-sabaki* and charging in with fleeting swiftness.

Kihon ippon

1. Acquire the skill to counter powerfully using the basic techniques.

2. Learn the relation between blocking and decisive technique.

3. Learn how to make use of fixed *maai*, the distance in which an attack can be delivered and the distance in which a block can become a decisive counterattack.

4. In relation to the distance and posture at the time of blocking, develop the instant judgment to counterattack swiftly by selecting the appropriate decisive technique (*kime-waza*).

5. Master the timing of blocking. This means seeing through the opponent's movements completely, waiting until the last possible moment, and blocking fast and sharply.

6. Learn to make good use of the various stances when blocking.

Jiyū ippon

1. This is the transitional stage to jiyū kumite, so the ultimate objectives of karate-dō—*goshin, jissen*; self-defense, actual combat—must be clearly recognized and training must be deadly serious.

2. With distancing at one's own discretion, this is attacking and defending in a practical way. Acquire the skill of decisively blocking in one breath (*ichibyōshi*).

3. Learn to effectively take advantage of chance, though it occurs only once.

4. Master the methods of effective counterattack, strong decisive techniques, changing techniques, leg movements and *tai-sabaki*.

Jiyū kumite

1. Investigate and become skilled in such matters as taking advantage of *maai*, which changes endlessly; leading the opponent into a *maai* favorable to oneself, and catching the opponent while dealing with his attack.

2. Learn *kake* and *kuzushi*.

3. Study the ways of catching and using chance.

4. Practice changing techniques and continuous techniques.

5. Gain an appreciation of the secret of converting defense into offense.

6. Study taking the initiative later (*go no sen*, see Vol. 3).

7. Study taking the initiative earlier (*sen no sen*, see Vol. 3).

8. Learn to evaluate situations, for example, recognize preparedness and unpreparedness, separate truth from falsehood.

9. Study continuous techniques and *tai-sabiki*.

10. Make the most of yourself. Devote yourself single-mindedly to serious study and training.

PREPARING FOR COMBAT

Understanding Training

From those who mastered the spirit of budō (matial arts), certain secret principles have been handed down from generation to generation. I introduce here a selection from these writings, which serve as a guide for training in kumite. Their practical application in deciding the issue of victory or defeat is not their only purpose; through them, one should come in contact with the spirit of the martial arts and judge himself. It remains then to practice karate-dō often and hard.

Keiko no mokuteki   *The purpose of training*
The ultimate purpose of training is to have the body perfectly habituated to the basic techniques. Then in actual combat, accurate techniques and movements are possible without conscious effort.

Yagyū Munenori, *Heihoka densho*

Tatakai no Yōtei   *Cardinal Points of Combat*

Kokoro wa karada ni tsurezu   *Mind and body: Neither*
karada wa kokoro ni tsurezu   *should be led by the other*
Whether in normal times or in combat, the mind should not change the least bit. Attentiveness should never relax, but a position should not be taken recklessly. The mind should be candidly open and judge without bias. Take care that the mind does not stop in one place but roves quietly over all things.

When the body is quiet, the mind should not be at a standstill; when the body is moving vigorously, the mind should be serene. The mind should not be dragged by the body. The body should not be dragged by the mind. Always, even when taking a position cautiously, move the body positively.

In enriching your mind, it won't do to leave in it any idle thoughts. And while letting your outward appearance seem pliant, it is imperative to be strong. in your heart of hearts and never let others penetrate your real intentions.

Miyamoto Musashi, *Gorin no sho*

I o motte teki ni gasshi   Meet the enemy with dignity,
sei o motte teki ni katsu   defeat him with strength

Whatever the circumstances, dignity does not change. Preparing correctly and boldly, not yielding to the enemy's movements—this is called dignity. The enemy can be brought under control without moving oneself.

Overwhelming the enemy with one's own movements is strength. Within the calm of dignity are hidden a thousand changes. The movement of strength can cope with ten thousand changes. In essence, dignity and strength are one.

Kotōda Yahei, *Ittōsai sensei kempō sho*

Teki ni yotte tenka seyo   Meeting the enemy

Make the techniques and tactics the enemy is trying to use your own. Strength against strength, pliancy against pliancy. If he strikes, block; if he blocks, disengage. It is said that in responses yielding to the enemy's advantage there are infinite changes.

Answer regular attacking tactics with the same, a surprise attack with a surprise attack. Even if you have the capability of fighting with bold regular tactics, use surprise. Or while giving the impression of a surprise attack, change to a regular tactic.

This is the opposite of what has been described as the ordinary way of fighting: if the enemy's methods are formal, use surprise; if he uses surprise, respond with formal methods. The secret of surprise versus formal methods and their relationship is surely one of the subtle points of combat.

Kotōda Yahei, *Ittōsai sensei kempō sho*

Kamae   *Posture*

Kamayuru to omowazu kiru   Without thinking of kamae,
koto nari to omoubeshi   think of cutting

The secret of the art of war has been said to be the perfection of the *chūdan-gamae*. Or that it is best to take one of the five postures—*jōdan, chūdan, gedan, migi waki* [right side], *hidari waki* [left side]—according to time and opponent.

While postures may be divided into five, the purpose is one. Whatever the posture, taking it is not an aim in itself; the purpose is to cut a person. Blocking the enemy's sword, hitting, striking, cutting him are all means to achieve the purpose. Means and the objective must not be confused.

Miyamoto Musashi, *Gorin no sho*

Kamae atte kamae nashi　　*Kamae: it exists, it doesn't exist*

Lower a *jōdan-gamae* slightly and it becomes *chūdan*. Raise a *chūdan* slightly in response to necessity and it becomes *jōdan*. Raise a *gedan* slightly, according to circumstances, and it becomes *chūdan*. If circumstances call for it, facing slightly toward the center changes *migi waki* or *hidari waki* into *chūdan* or *gedan*.

Miyamoto Musashi, *Gorin no sho*

Me no Kubari　　　　　　　　　　　　　Using the Eyes

Heihō no metsuki　　　　　　　　　*The eyes in combat*

It is important to keep the eyes on all things, seeing both widely and deeply.

In seeing things, there are *kan* and *ken*. Penetrating the true nature of things is *kan*; seeing surface phenomena is *ken*.

Accurately judging faraway conditions and rightly grasping the nature of nearby phenomena is a secret principle of the art of war. The secret of success is to know the enemy's sword without looking at it, to concretely assess his nature, and to not be seduced by his movements.

It is vitally essential to take in both sides (left and right) without moving the eyeballs. Mastery of this is not easy.

Miyamoto Musashi, *Gorin no sho*

Ma　　　　　　　　　　　　　　　　　　Distancing

Kokoro ni ma o tomezu　　　*Mind and distance: neither*
ma ni kokoro o tomezu　　　*should arrest the other*

Ma [distancing] is the key to victory. However, if you enter battle with good distancing, as a matter of course, the enemy will do likewise.

In our style of fighting, calculating *ma* is not simply a matter of distance and space but of taking advantage of the relationship of energy and power and the rhythm of distancing. No matter what dangers there are to be feared, seize any opening without vacillation, and snatch the initiative in a life-and-death struggle. If the mind is caught up in *ma*, free movement is impossible. If the mind is not preoccupied about *ma*, correct distancing will be taken without fail. When neither *ma* arrests mind nor mind arrests *ma*, all changes can be answered naturally, and the sphere of no-thought will be attained.

Ma is not just the difference between near and far. Seeing through all conditions of change, not letting the opponent take the initiative, always holding the advantage and advancing the fight are the cardinal points of *ma* in life.

Kotōda Yahei, *Ittōsai sensei kempō sho*

Chansu o Ikasu — Making the Most of Chance

Kao mo agesasezu uchi ni utte — *Striking, not letting the opponent raise his face*

Whether it seems that bringing down the opponent with one blow is possible or impossible, drive in repeatedly without letting him raise his head. Chances for victory are rare. To not let the one chance escape, to win with certainty, continue striking intensely until the enemy is demolished, body and mind.

Yagyū Munenori, *Heihōka densho*

Semekomi — Attacking

Munen musō no uchi — *No ideas-no thoughts strike*

The opponent is about to strike. You are ready to strike. Your body comes to the attitude of striking. Your mind concentrates on striking. Your arm is at its most natural. With acceleration, great strength, swiftness, the strike is made. This is the most important, *munen musō* [free of all ideas and thoughts] strike. To attain it, training must be carried to the limit.

Miyamoto Musashi, *Gorin no sho*

Sekka no atari — *Lightning strike*

The lightning strike is this. When the enemy's sword and your sword come to the point of almost touching, without raising your sword the least bit, you charge in with maximum strength. Strong legs, strong body, strong arms—these three strengths must be combined and the strike made with celerity. This is not possible unless training is incessant.

Miyamoto Musashi, *Gorin no sho*

Hyōshi — Rhythm

Hyōshi o kokoroete — *Understand rhythm,*
shōri o tsukamu — *capture victory*

There is rhythm in all things. Music and dance have their harmonious and gentle rhythms. In the martial arts, in archery, in shooting, in riding a horse—all have rhythm and timing. The rhythm of arts and techniques can never be ignored, but especially in the martial arts, rhythm must be mastered through training.

The rhythms of the art of war are various. First of all it is necessary to make a distinction between those that are appropriate and those that are not, and from among large and small, slow and fast, to know those that are compatible with one's aims. Knowing the rhythms of distancing and of the opponent is a crucial point. Especially, if one does not master reverse rhythm, his training is only half complete.

In combat, know the enemy's rhythm, use a rhythm he cannot anticipate, upset his rhythm, and win.

Miyamoto Musashi, Gorin no sho

Hyōshi o kuruwasete katsu   *Upset rhythm, win*

If the enemy uses his sword with a large rhythm, use a small rhythm. Counter his small rhythm with a large rhythm. Understanding how to make your rhythm different from the enemy's is the important point, for if the rhythms are the same, it will be easier for him to use his sword. Winning by intentionally upsetting the enemy's rhythm and tempo is the secret of combat.

Yagyū Munenori, Heihōka densho

2
KUZUSHI
LEG SWEEP

KUZUSHI, LEG SWEEP

Keinosuke Enoeda has a reputation for achievements that stir the imagination. Using the power of thoroughly strengthened legs and loins, he delivers strikes and kicks of great force, which cannot be blocked easily with simple evasive tactics. His *ashi barai* (leg sweep), which uses the whole body, is very strong. Especially amazing is his ability to cut in deeply, catch his opponent's rear supporting leg, and send him flying.

Chance and timing are crucial factors in the *ashi barai* and *kuzushi* (crushing the enemy). No matter how good one's aim is, if the opponent's posture is well balanced and reliable and his stance is steady, one may not be able to penetrate them and may end up being defeated himself. One effective way is to lead the opponent and catch the moment at the beginning of his movement when the shifting of the center of gravity makes his balance very delicate. This requires excellent timing. Again, when the opponent is responding to your attack, there may be any opening for *kuzushi*. Or an *ashi barai* can be effective when the opponent charges in, his front leg stops, and there is the instant when his center of gravity comes over his front ankle. Another powerfully effective way is to pounce on the moment when the opponent settles down and cut in (*karikomi*) deeply.

As shown by his past record, Enoeda has mastered these tactics, and many an opponent has tasted the cup of defeat. He could not have reached his present level without abundant, fundamental training of legs and hips day by day.

In the pictures on the following pages, Enoeda's opponent is Fujikiyo Ōmura, an up-and-coming karateka with good hand techniques, good leg techniques and good prospects.

1

2

3

4

5

6

1

2

4

5

Two-leg sweep When pressing in on the opponent and he is just at the point of withdrawing, this is a very strong leg sweep. Use front and back legs together to cut him down. It is hard to evade this tactic.

7

Powerful leg sweep At the moment the opponent tries to evade your strike, slide in and press the back of his knee with your kneecap. At the same time this movement is stopped, put your foot deep behind his ankle.

1

3

Powerful leg sweep With your leg behind the opponent's knee to arrest his movement, execute a straight punch to the face when he is off balance. This is not actually *ashi barai* but is equally effective.

2

4

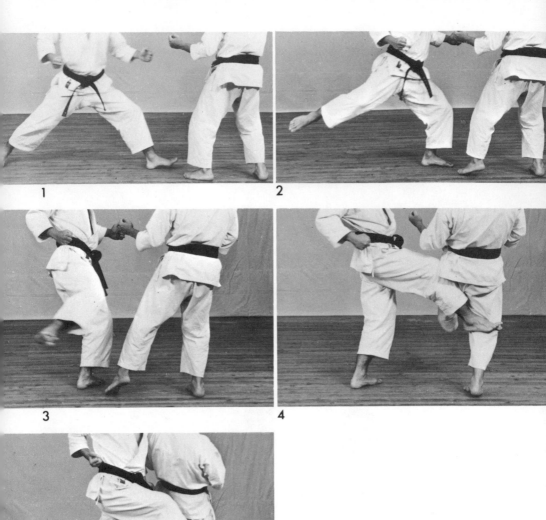

Swinging the legs in ashi barai The point is timing; execution must come just when the opponent withdraws his hips and shifts his center of gravity. With your hips low, support your body weight firmly on the front leg, putting power in the back ankle. Strike the back of his knee.

Back heel sweep When you are driving in for a lunge punch, the opponent changes to *hanmi*. Stretch your front leg to his back ankle. While cutting with the foot, push his chest with the striking arm. The foot sweep (inward) and the arm push (outward) must be done at the same time.

Second International Amateur Karate Federation Tournament, Tokyo, 1977

3
CHANGING TECHNIQUES

CHANGING TECHNIQUES

Toru Yamaguchi's movements are rhythmical and brilliantly nimble; his techniques have the sharpness of a keen-edged sword. Leading the opponent to expect a kick, then taking him by surprise by leaping high and punching or striking is just one example of an endless series of changes it is impossible to be on guard against. Though seemingly unplanned, such tactics are never that; they come from calculating all possibilities imaginable.

With only a barely perceptible movement of arms or legs, he may dissipate the force of an opponent's strike, responding with a counter technique without delay. Or he will catch the instant for a counterattack by seizing the tiniest of openings, throwing the opponent into confusion, and delivering a jolting technique.

There is ingenuity, too, in his *kamae*. He can bring pressure to bear on the strongest of opponents by the boldness of his expression. Or with a humorous expression, he can gently lead the opponent and wrap him up at his own pace.

After twenty years of training, Yamaguchi is an expert among experts. His ability to read the opponent's movements in advance, to execute continuous techniques quickly, appropriately and with precision is the result of daily, accumulative training in basics.

Even at the very beginning of training, executing techniques in a halfway fashion is ineffective. It is necessary that they be carried out decisively in conformity with body movements.

In the pictures on the following pages, Yamaguchi's opponent is Yoshiki Satō. A leading karateka of the Tohoku region (northern Japan), his large-scale techniques are stimulatingly executed.

2

3

1

4

5

6

1

2

3

Changing techniques While suppressing a reverse punch, stop the opponent's movement with your right fist to his inside knee. Sweep away further attacks with a rising right fist; finish with a left close punch.

4

5

Crescent sweep After blocking a middle level straight punch with your leg, reverse direction, change legs, counterattack with back kick.

4

5

6

Jumping counterattack Against an upper level attack, jump high and strike to the face, in the excellent way shown here.

3

4

1

2

5

6

Counterattack by stopping the opponent's movement Just when the opponent launches a fierce attack, lower your body by crossing your knees, change your *kamae* hand, and strike his knee lightly. Don't consciously strike forcefully to break his posture. Striking lightly is the important point. Against further strikes, use a sweeping left-hand block.

3

4

7

8

9

10

1

2   3

6   7

Crescent kick-block, back kick Timing the move carefully, deflect the opponent's kick with a *mikazuki-geri* (crescent kick). From that position, turn full around, change legs, and deliver a back kick. In turning around, the most important point is that the body weight comes completely onto the supporting leg.

4

5

8

9

10

Essential points of the crescent kick Body weight must ride
fully on the front leg. Hips must not rise. The knee must swing
high and close to the body. Deflect the opponent's wrist with
the sole. Kick in line with the opponent's extended arm.

Changing legs according to maai When the opponent's penetration is deep, the kicking leg should come down behind the supporting leg. (*Left photos.*) When not deep, it should come down a little in front of the supporting leg. (*Right photos.*)

Jumping counterattack Jumping depends on the spring of the knees and ankles. Since the time margin for deeply bending the knees and using their spring power is limited, the spring of the ankles must be utilized to the maximum. Bring the knees high, close to the chest.

4
CUTTING KICK

CUTTING KICK

There are very few competitors who can use both hands and both legs with as much skill as Masahiko Tanaka. In his attacks, striking and kicking are always combined. Principal weapons are roundhouse strikes and roundhouse kicks; an exceedingly effective technique against big, hard-to-reach opponents is a sharp, skillful *kizami-geri* (cutting kick) executed with the front foot.

Snap is necessary in kicking. Without the benefit of snap, even an *oshikomi-geri* (pressing-in kick) will have little force. Unless the spring of the knee is tempered through daily training, a strong, commanding kick is impossible. But getting the body accustomed to not changing the height of the hips and not bending the hips while raising the kneecap to chest level is not easy training. Besides that, there are the important points of bending the ankle of the supporting leg deeply, having the sole firmly press the floor for the momentary maintenance of balance and effectively applying the spring of kicking ankle, knee and hip.

Tanaka's technique of suddenly switching front and back legs and executing a cutting kick, seen in tournaments from time to time, is beautiful. But he did not start out by being naturally skillful. He overcame many trials, practiced without complaining, and gradually approached the point where he could have the feeling of using arms and legs with near perfection. Witnessing this was gratifying, and I hope that a great number of the younger followers of karate-dō will discover the secret of it.

In the pictures on the following pages, Tanaka's opponent is Masao Kawazoe.

1

2

3

Cutting kick Withdraw the front leg in a wide motion and check the opponent's back-fist strike. From that posture, execute a sharp kick with the front leg for a strong counterattack.

60

4

5

6

1

2

From punch to cutting kick   Finding an opening, drive in for a
straight punch. Catching the moment when the opponent withdraws, let fly with a kick with the front leg for another attack.

3

4

Leading opponent and kicking Entice the opponent into advancing by sliding back the front foot, then use it for a small sharp roundhouse kick. This is very effective, but only if snap is fully used and balance is very good.

Changing feet and kicking Without withdrawing the hips, withdraw the front leg, immediately change legs and kick. (*Upper photos.*) The feeling should be of withdrawing the leg slightly. If the hips are withdrawn, the kick will not be effective. (*Lower photos.*) Lift the kicking knee high.

1　2

3　4

5　6

Withdrawing leg, cutting kick　Lead the opponent by withdrawing the front leg. When the distance is right, suddenly raise knee and kick. From the beginning of the kick to the end the body weight must ride firmly on the supporting leg.

Changing feet While drawing back the front foot, induce the opponent into making a lunge punch. Execute a cutting kick at the appropriate time and distance. Though the leg withdraws the hips must not, and the posture must not change.

1   2

5   6

9   10

Cutting kick after block To deal with the opponent's lunge punch, draw the front leg well back. While blocking his backfist, make a cutting kick with the front leg. Posture when blocking and when kicking are the same. Hips must not draw back.

3

4

7

8

11

1

2

3

4

Cutting kick after attack When the opponent retreats from your charging in for a lunge punch, bring the back leg forward, make a cutting kick with the front leg. Bringing the leg forward and raising the kicking knee must be done at the same time to catch the instant when *maai* is best.

5

7

6

8

1

2

3

Using the ankle Besides sharp snap in raising the knee, the tensing of the ankle and toes of the kicking leg is critical for the *kizami-geri*, to give it the force to break through a partial block and reach the target. The instep is also used for this kick, but only rarely.

5
RESPONSES

RESPONSE TO PUNCH AND KICK

Masao Kawazoe and Yoshiharu Ōsaka are both men in full possession of techniques that are correct and harmonious with basic techniques. Kawazoe is especially noted for his kicks, which are strong, good, effective and have a sharp snap, while Ōsaka is especially noted for his strikes, which are fast, far-reaching and heavy. They have excellent records in many tournaments.

Immediately after furious mutual attacks, responding with strikes or kicks that require a change of posture is exceedingly difficult, because balance is easily disrupted. As might be expected when training has really taken hold, these two keep their form from becoming disorganized and their decisive power from losing vigor while executing any number of techniques. Just seeing them face to face with each other is quite a sight.

In a contest, it is not good to be swayed by insignificant wins or loses. The fundamental techniques mastered through daily, hard training should be used freely, fully and effectively. The point not to be forgotten is to go through to final victory.

1

2

3

4

5

6

7

8

9

10

11

12

1

3

2

Striking simultaneously   Kawazoe's powerful kick is aimed at
the instant Ōsaka makes a strong punch. Kawazoe's front kick,
utilizing the power of the hips to the fullest, is masterful.

4

5

Striking simultaneously   Both men attack fiercely at the same time with reverse punches, but both are slightly short of the target. Changing feet, both punch again but, short of the target, withdraw.

3

4

5

1

2

Striking simultaneously Both men attack at the same time. Ōsaka's flowing block with the right palm slightly but effectively deflects Kawazoe's fist. He then hits Ōsaka's jaw skillfully with his fore-fist. Changing feet and maintaining perfect balance is the height of skill.

3

4

Second International Amateur Karate Federation Tournament, Tokyo, 1977

6
LAST-CHANCE TECHNIQUE

LAST-CHANCE TECHNIQUE

Mikio Yahara is a karateka whose daredevil style of fighting in the midst of a heated contest leaves spectators breathless—somersaulting out of danger, reversing direction completely to turn defense into offense and so on. Though his forte has been kicking, he uses his limbs freely and appropriately in a great variety of techniques. As can be seen from his splendid record, he can bring an opponent under control with strikes or punches or kicks.

When it looks as though he is about to dispose of an opponent with a strike, he will suddenly change to a back-fist strike or other techniques of continuous attack. In response to the opponent's movement, distancing and posture, a strike may become a punch or kick. Such skillfulness is always the result of hard, daily training, in which the proper use of *tai-sabaki* and techniques are accumulated little by little into the fundamentals of movement.

Yahara's adroitness in seizing on chance and boldly applying *kani-basami* (crab claws) is extraordinary. This is a *sutemi waza* (last-chance technique). It is inconceivable that this comes from a half-hearted movement; determination is essential. It is a great achievement to be able to do this, but it is only possible in a do-or-die frame of mind.

In the pictures on the following pages, Yahara's opponent is Takashi Naito. He has learned to perform briskly and well and has a bright future.

1

2

3

4

5

6

Crab claws While lightly blocking the opponent's punching
arm with the right palm, the body is turned around for a sharp
back elbow strike. Seeing this is ineffective, one arm goes to
the floor behind the opponent. Catch his chest with the right
foot, scoop the back of his knee with the left. Besides excellent
reflexes, this requres accumulated training.

1 2

5 6

Back roundhouse kick While going in for a front-kick attack, leave the kicking foot where it is, and while turning around, make a daring back roundhouse kick. Determination and balance are the essentials.

3

4

7

1

4

5

8

9

High and low Facing a front kick, jump over the opponent, turn, and while dodging under his roundhouse kick, counter with your own kick.

2　　　　　　　　3

6　　　　　　　　7

Turning for back elbow strike With the front leg supporting the body weight use it as a pivot and rotate the hips like a top (*mawarikomu*). Turning legs only is not effective. Keeping the hips at the same level as one leg is the sine qua non for balance.

Essential points of crab claws Use left leg for support and swing right leg from the front. At the same time, put hand on floor. While your body falls, use both legs like scissors, the left against the back of the opponent's legs, right against his chest. This requires instantaneous judgment.

Sliding in   Aiming at the instant the opponent kicks, slide in by lowering the body. At the same time, kick for *kime*. The feeling should be of resolving to ram your head into his crotch. Simply sinking the body to avoid the kick has no effect.

7
CONTINUOUS TECHNIQUES

CONTINUOUS TECHNIQUES

Hiroshi Shōji is one of the small number of karateka who form a link between the old and new generations in karate-dō. He has mastered the "real combat," fundamental techniques, which are supported by a long tradition, but also belongs to the world of tournament karate, which comes like a fresh breeze. As a competitor, he has won kata championships twice and has an excellent record.

The techniques he has mastered are correct, reliable, sharp and decisive, the essence of karate techniques. In kumite, he is very impressive, using basic techniques speedily, forcefully and freely in all directions. He will suddenly stamp in from a distance and attack with vigorous, large-scale techniques. When this is not effective, he will slide deep in and switch to back-fist strikes, elbow strikes or other small-scale techniques without giving the opponent time to recover. Sharp vertical movements, quick movements to the side, smooth turning movements, *tai-sabaki* and other body movements are all superb. His breathing at the moment of delivering a technique is also exemplary.

In the pictures on the following pages, Shōji's opponent is Toru Yamaguchi.

1

4

5

6

7

2

3

1

2

3

Leg sweep inside outward Deal with the opponent's reverse punch by turning the hips and executing a straight punch at the same time. When this seems ineffective use back leg to sweep his front knee inside outward. He cannot help but fall. This is a strong surprise technique.

4

5

6

1

2

3

Changing legs and striking Reverse punches are strong but
indecisive for either side. Instantly change feet for a decisive
back-fist strike. As seen here, the position of the body, balance
and timing of the technique while changing feet show the skill
of veteran karateka.

4

5

6

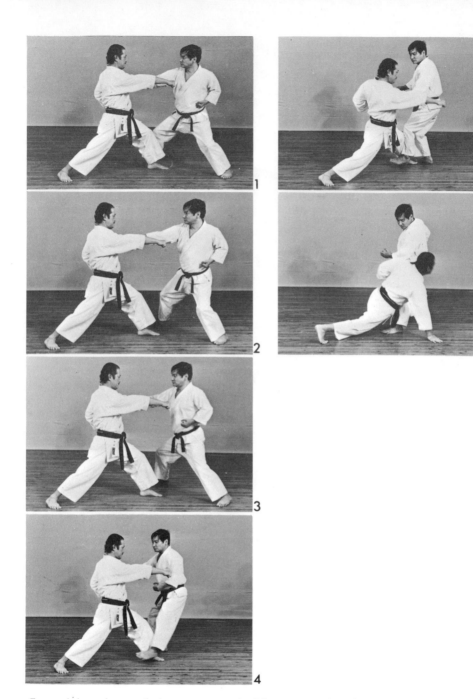

Essential points of leg sweep, inside outward After an exchange of punches, the front foot stamps slightly to the outside, and the rear foot flies out to catch the opponent's ankle. The movement of the supporting leg and the leg sweep must be simultaneous. Hitting the ankle at a low point is best.

Changing feet and striking   After indecisive punches, quickly withdraw front foot, change feet, change posture while sliding foot forward for back-fist strike. Besides balance, not withdrawing the hips with the leg is crucial. Doing so changes *maai*, leaving one open to attack.

Training in changing feet, striking   When withdrawing, position of hips must not change. When striking, back foot must stand firmly, hips must thrust forward, and movement of withdrawing hand must be sufficiently large.

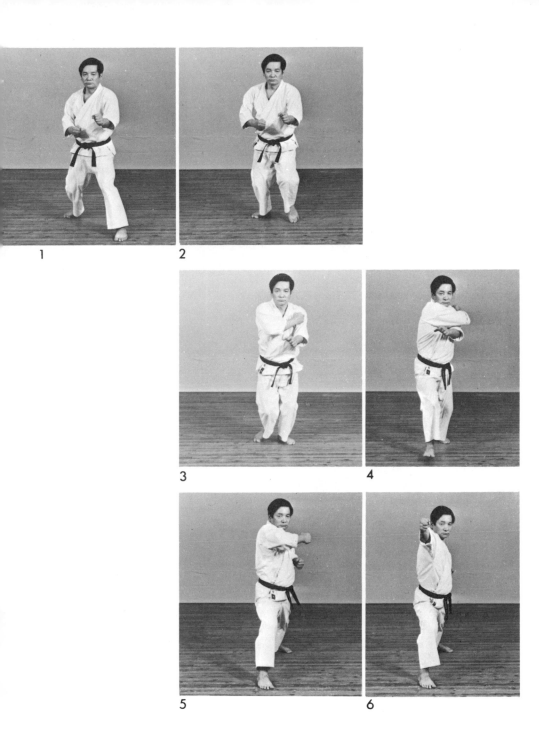

1

2

3

4

5

6

Training in leg sweep, inside outward Body weight must be on the back leg. Use the sole of the front foot as though sweeping the floor. Bring it back in an upward motion. If the height of the hips changes, balance will be lost.

8
BLOCKING KIME

BLOCKING KIME

The real blocking techniques of karate do not end simply with the blocking of an attack; according to the way the block is used, it can be a strong *kime-waza* (decisive technique). *Uke kime ichijo*: *Uke* and *kime* are one. This is the characteristic that, more than any other, gives karate-dō its distinctive nature. With only a block, arms and legs forged into iron by daily training can deliver a tremendous shock to an opponent and shatter his will to fight.

To be able to protect oneself without injuring human life is the very soul of karate-dō and can be said to be the proper function of all martial arts.

In recent years, contests have become popular everywhere. Great importance is attached to gaining points by concentrating one's energies on *henka waza, renzoku waza, tai-sabaki, deai* etc., and to making great progress through skill. This is fine so long as the spirit of karate is not lost. If it is lost, there is cause for great sorrow.

In former times, when karate was thought of as fighting techniques, there was the motto, *ikken hisatsu*, to kill with one blow. The meaning that *uke* is also *kime* is implicit in this motto.

We must pay great attention to this point, conduct contests with seriousness, understand the nature of karate-dō, and pass these things on to those who follow karate-dō in the future.

In the pictures on the following pages, my opponent is Yoshiharu Ōsaka.

Uke wa kime nari   The block becomes the decisive technique. This is the motto of Shōtō-kan karate-dō. According to its use the block can become a strong attack. Along with advancing the leg and posture, the important point is decisiveness.

1

2

3

4

1

2

3

4

1

2

3

Suppressing attack When an attack is aimed at your solar plexus, catch the moment it starts. From the flowing water position (*mizu-nagare kamae*, see Vol. 2), press down on the opponent's striking arm and strike him in the abdomen.

1

2

1

2

3

Sword hand block, elbow strike   Against a middle level attack, slide in one step. From inside the attacking arm, while cutting the eyes with the fingernails, rotate the arm and block the opponent's wrist. Immediately make a front elbow strike to his solar plexus. This is all part of the ordinary sword hand block.

4

5

6

1

2

Middle level block, outside inward, elbow strike   Slide in one step and swing the fist from the outside, striking just below the nose. Continue by blocking with a strike to the arm. From that position, strike with the elbow. It is important to execute the technique while swinging the arm in a large circle.

3

4

5

6

1

2

Side elbow strike While sliding swiftly into *hanmi*, parry the
opponent's punching arm and strike below his armpit with the
elbow.

Sliding block, punch   With a motion as if extending the elbow inside the attacking arm, use two-finger spear hand or fore-fist against eyes or the point just below the nose.

Rising block, stick hand strike   To plunge into range of an attack takes spirit. Keep hips low, back foot strongly supporting and body facing diagonally. You must still have the power to strike to the side of the body with the stick hand (*shubō*) or elbow. Bending hips or leaning is fatal.

1

2

3

4

5

1   2

5   6

Roundhouse sword hand block   At the onset of the opponent's attack, slide the front leg into *hangetsu* (half-moon) shape. At the same time, shift weight to the front leg and swing the sword hand. From that position, block the punching arm. While drawing the opponent in, rotate the hips and attack with the elbow. Swing the sword hand in harmony with the hip rotation.

3

4

7

8

Suppressing attack To suppress an attack, it is necessary to act just when the opponent attacks, thus necessary to have the resolution to engage in simultaneous attacks. End the confrontation quickly with a forceful strike to the opponent's elbow using the stick hand.

1

2

3

4

5

1

2

4

5

Sliding block punch When the opponent is at the point of attacking, slide as if to the inside of his attacking arm, straighten the elbow for a decisive fist or spear hand to the face. It is important to thrust the hips forward boldly while coming into the half-front-facing position.

3

6

1

2

3

4

Training in roundhouse sword hand block From *hanmi*, slide
the front foot in the *hangetsu* shape. While taking a front stance
(weight on the front leg), swing the sword hand widely from
the inside in conjunction with the rotation of the hips. At the
same time, execute *kime* with right fist or elbow.

5

6 7

1

2   3   4

Training in roundhouse block, outside inward While sliding
the back foot a big step forward, swing the right fist in a big
circle in conjunction with the rotation of the hips. Bend the
elbow for middle level block. While coming into straddle-leg
stance, execute *kime* with elbow strike.

5   6

7

GLOSSARY

age-uke shubō uchi: rising block, stick hand strike, 130
ai-uchi: striking simultaneously, 78 80, 82, 134
ashi barai: leg sweep, 26, 32, 34, 36
ashi fumikae: changing legs, 55, 65, 67, 82, 108, 112, 114

budō : martial arts, 20, 118

choku-zuki: straight punch, 34, 46, 62, 106
chōyaku hangeki: jumping counter-attack, 48, 56
chūdan-gamae: middle level posture, 21
chūdan soto uke: middle level block, outside inward, 126

deai, 118
deai osae: suppressing attack, 122, 134

gedan-gamae: lower level posture, 21
go no sen: taking the initiative later, 17, 19
goshin: self-defense, 18
gyaku-zuki: reverse punch, 44, 80, 106, 108

hangetsu kata: half-moon shape, 132, 138
hanmi: half-front-facing position, 16, 37, 128, 136, 138
henka waza: changing techniques, 118
hidari waki-gamae: left side posture, 21
hiji-ate: elbow strike, 124, 126
hiki-te: withdrawing hand, 114
hyōshi: rhythm, 23

ichibyōshi: in one breath, 18
ikken hissatsu: to kill with one blow, 11, 118

jissen: actual fighting, 14, 15, 102

jōdan-gamae: upper level posture, 21

kake, 18
kamae: posture, 14, 17, 21, 40
kamaekata: 16
kan, 22
kani-basami: crab claws, 86, 90, 99
karikomi: cutting in, 26
ken, 22
kime: finish, 11, 15, 100, 138
kime-waza: decisive technique, 18, 118
kizami-geri: cutting kick, 58–72
kokyū: breathing (rhythm), 15, 102
kuzushi: crushing (the enemy), 18, 26

maai (ma): distancing, 15, 16, 18, 22, 55, 70, 112
mae hiji-ate: front elbow strike, 124
mawarikomi: turning (like a top), 98
mawashi-geri: roundhouse kick, 64, 96
mawashi shutō uke: roundhouse sword hand block, 132, 138
me no tsukekata: fixing the eyes, 16
migi waki-gamae: right side posture, 21
mikazuki barai: crescent sweep, 46
mikazuki-geri: crescent kick, 52, 54
mikazuki-geri barai: crescent kick-block, 52
mizu-nagare kamae: flowing water position, 122
moroashi-gari: two-leg sweep, 37
munen musō: free of all ideas and thoughts, 23

nagashi-uke: flowing block, 82

oi-zuki: lunge punch, 37, 67, 68, 70
oshikomi-geri: pressing-in kick, 58

randori: sparring in judo, 15
renzoku waza: continuous techniques, 118

142